Broadband Speed;

How To Increase Router Speed, Solving Broadband Speed Problems, Internet Router Connections, Cabling Data Sockets, Moving The Broadband Router, Installation, Data Cable

By

Martin Laurence

Table of Contents

1. Introduction to Broadband Problems

Firstly thank you very much for purchasing 'Broadband Speed.' This book is designed to be an easy to follow guide for trouble-shooting your Internet speed problems and get you running at maximum download and upload speed. I will cover the extensive problems that cause slowdowns on Broadband and provide solutions to make sure you are using your Internet speed to its full potential. I'm focusing on hardware, cabling and Router positioning. Some of the resolutions are relatively inexpensive such as a problem with your line, and some if you so desire could be more costly such as networking your house. But I explain it in a simple manner so that whatever option you want to do, you can do this yourself.

Chronically slow Broadband speed can be incredibly infuriating. The reasons can be as simply as a faulty filter, your line provider or a problem with your Wi-Fi.

Firstly we'll check your actual line quality and then move onto looking at your house architecture as this could be slowing you down. The options then are moving your Router which I explain and also cabling a hard-wired link to a PC or MAC. These options will depend on how you use the internet. If you predominately use Wi-Fi and your Router is stuck at the front of the house and you're at the rear then moving the Router could be the best solution. If on the other hand you barely use Wi-Fi but use a PC or Mac in an office then you could run a Cat5e link from the Router straight to your Computer. The speed difference could be amazing since walls and ceilings etc cause huge slowdowns.

Wi-Fi can be as slow as 50% when compared to hard-wired networks – and sometimes a lot worse.

The Stats:
Wi-Fi can be as slow as 300mbps right down to 54mbps
Hard-Wired Cat5e Cable can be as fast as 1000mbps
Hard-Wired Cat6A Cable an be as fast as 10,000mbps

So that's where a direct hard-wired link from your Router to your computer will triumph every single time. This works exactly the same if you have a smart TV that has a very slow connection. You're putting a lot of strain on your Wi-Fi if you're downloading TV series and films.

So the number 1 thing to do before we even get into the rest of the book is to check our Broadband speed right now. With everything as it is, whatever you're using – Wi-Fi or Hard-Wiring. You can go onto websites like 'Speed Checker' and it will tell you your maximum upload and download speed.

This is a barometer for us to know where we stand right now and gives us a guide as to how much we can improve.

Write both numbers down. Okay done that? We now have our current speed - now let's improve it!

2. Line Quality

Before we look at the Router, Filters or even consider cabling anything extra, we need to start with your line. The analogue side of the Broadband is an indication of your line health - is it working perfectly. Any issues with line quality will affect your Broadband speed. No matter how good the rest of the network and equipment is - a problem with your line will bring everything down.

Is the Line working?

So firstly let's check the line quality. Firstly does your line work? Sounds a stupid question right? But i know many people who don't use the voice side of their Broadband anymore because they have a mobile phone and only use the Internet side of the line. So this means the speech side is never used and they have no idea whether it's good or not. I've had a couple of instances where the Broadband side of the line works to an extent but the speech side is completely dead. This is because the data side can work on one leg - albeit badly while the voice side needs two legs - two wires to work properly. So test the line, use a normal phone that you know works - make sure you have an ADSL filter plugged in to the socket too. Simply pick up the handset and you should have dial tone.

Line Quality

Secondly is there any crackling noises or breaking up on the line? We want to test that the line is clean and clear, by that i mean we don't want to hear any funny noises at all when listening to dial tone. We want a nice crisp dial tone. If you can hear any crackling, or the line cutting out then you have an issue.

Poor Quality?

If you can hear a crackling noise - unplug everything else from the network - Smart TV, other phones, and including Router. We want to eliminate your equipment as a possible problem. Take your phone to the first line box - the main telephone socket that comes into the house. Don't forget a filter too and try again. If the line is clear then one of your pieces of equipment is faulty and could be slowing down your Broadband. So you will have to plug each of your pieces of equipment one at time and keep checking the phone line. You should be able to eliminate the problem by doing this. I once had an automated home oil control causing a problem. This records your house oil level and automatically calls a company to deliver more when levels are low. But it had gone faulty and once removed bought speed levels back to normal. So check the line again - if it's all good then you're good to move on otherwise:

Still have a problem?

So with everything unplugged and still having a line problem then you have a faulty line and you need to contact your line provider. When you call up to say you have a fault, say you have unplugged everything - this is usually the first thing they ask!

Once your line is repaired we can move on.

3. Checking Your Optimal Speed

So we have checked our line and it's working perfectly fine. Great! So onto testing the top speed of the Broadband now.

We have already tested the current speed right at the start of the book. Now we want to test the optimal speed. To do this we take our computer/laptop (ideally) to the first line box again where we tested the line quality. Plug the Router back in and switch it on. Now we want to plug a patch lead into the Router and into your computer/laptop. This is so we have a hard-wired link to the Router creating minimal loss of signal.

The Broadband will take about 5 minutes to see the Router so wait for all the lights to come back on and power up your computer.

Once you can see the Broadband is back on and your computer can see it, log on to the Broadband Speed Checker again and start it off. Ideally we want these figures to be faster than before. They should be a lot faster since you're plugging directly into the Router.

So now we have established that is your fastest speed - we now want to retain that speed throughout the house.

4. Hard-Wiring Vs Wi-Fi

There's two ways to retain your Broadband speed. One is to hard-wire from your Router to the places you use your Smart TV, your Laptop etc The other is to move your Router to a more central location within your house and maximize your Wi-Fi.

Did you know Wi-Fi is an incredibly ineffective way of using the Internet? In most cases it's the house that is the problem; thick walls, perhaps there's metal inside the construction, multiple floors, and/or you may simply may be out of range. This is common if your Router is at the front of the house and you're trying to use a computer at the rear of the house or even in an office in your shed. I've tried this and it's dreadful!

Wi-Fi can be as slow as 50% when compared to hard-wired networks – and sometimes a lot worse! So that's where a direct hard-wired link from your Router to your computer will triumph every single time. This works exactly the same if you have a smart TV that has a very slow connection. You're putting a lot of strain on your Wi-Fi if you're downloading TV series and films.

By cabling from your Router directly to a computer/TV/Laptop we utilize your broadband speed to its maximum. This is great for watching films, sending large files or simply surfing the net faster and more efficiently with no annoying dropouts.

However if the thought of hard-wiring from your Router isn't appealing or you mainly use tablets and smart phones etc then moving your Router is the next best thing.

In the following chapters I tell you how to do both so you can skip chapters if you're doing it one way or the other.

5. Using Only Wi-Fi and Maximising it

Before I go into cabling I thought I'd cover the other option which is if you're using Wi-Fi only. If you're using tablets or smart phones and you're smart TV's which use Wi-Fi and you don't want to hard-wire your network then you have two options:

- Maximise your Wi-Fi where is it
- Move your Router

Maximising your Wi-Fi is possible and includes simple things from buying a more powerful Router, making a simple sail to attack to the antenna to reflect more of the signal into your house to hacking your Router and increasing the signal.

I cover many of these simple tricks and more in an easy to understand book focusing purely on making your Wi-Fi more efficient:

How To Boost Wi-Fi Speed: DIY Hacks To Increase Speed

I've also had only the Wi-Fi go faulty on a few Routers too. Can you check this if you're suffering slow speeds? My laptop was terrible with W-Fi even when next to the Router. When I plugged it straight in with a lead it was perfect. So you need to phone your provider and they will post out a free Router. It's also worth bearing in mind that not all Routers are created equal. The free ones and cheap ones tend to be slightly slower than say some that are upwards of £100/$150.

Option two is move your Router to a more central location in the house. There's actually a number of reasons to move the Router:

- It's in a cosmetically unappealing place.
- The Router is at the front of the house and you're using your Wi-Fi at the rear.
- You want to maximize your Broadband speed and move the Router to your computer and plug in direct using a patch lead.

These three reasons and more are why you should move the Router.

A Wi-Fi signal spreads outward in a sphere so like cordless phones the signal actually works better when up higher or on another floor. Not only that many people are now moving their Router so it's situated next to their computer. They can use a patch lead and plug directly into it. This maximizes your Broadband so there is no loss of speed.

This is the same as cabling a hard-wired link to a computer that is further away but you use Cat5e cable.

So let's get onto the equipment we'll need to cable either the Router or a Hard-Wired data link to the computer.

6. Equipment Needed to Move Hard-Wire a Data link

I'm going to list the 'tools' that you will probably need, if you're cautious about spending money then it may be worth doing a 'dry run of the job' – looking at exactly where you're going to cable to and working out what you'll need to complete the job.

I'll also go into the actual equipment that you will need – cable – outlets. These are essential to making it work.

I'm sure once you've looked at the job, worked out your cable route, you will discover you don't need half of this equipment. Most of this equipment is available at your local hardware shop or on the internet, or even perhaps you can borrow the odd tool from a friend over a weekend to complete the work.

Basic Tools:
(Available from any tool centre)
Wire Cutters
Flat-blade Screwdriver
Phillips (cross-head) Screw Driver
Hammer - WHITE and BLACK cable clips

Raw plugs
Screws

Punch Down Tool connection tool (connecting the data socket modules)

Battery Drill
Masonry drill bit – 5mm
Wood Drill bit – 5mm

Power Drill (SDS is usually the best)
Mix of heavy Masonry drill bits

Clip-gun - plus clips
BLACK and CLEAR pack of Tie-Wraps
Electrical Tape - WHITE and BLACK

Step Ladder
Double/Triple extension Ladder - if you have two floors (these can be hired and are very inexpensive)

Data Equipment

This will need to be ordered as per the requirement of the job.

Cable:
(Available from an electrical Wholesalers/Online)

So you can use Cat5e which is perfectly workable for the average Broadband speed and Infinity etc, Cat6A gives it a longer life and some added future proofing.

Both comes in boxes of 300 meters so one box is more than enough for a typical house. You can buy black exterior Cat5e cable too if you're mainly cabling outside.

Hard-Wired Cat5e Cable can be as fast as 1000mbps
Hard-Wired Cat6A Cable can be as fast as 10,000mbps

Both Cat5e and Cat6A cable comes in boxes of 300 meters.

Socket Outlets
This what you will plug your computer into. There's a number of ways of connecting your computer - one is a mounted outlet and the other is crimping a RJ45 plug at each end.

I recommend installing a socket both ends and using a patch lead to connect to the Router and at the other end a patch lead connecting to the Computer/smart TV.

Why? It just keeps things really simple and is easier than crimping. You can of course crimp the cable, but cable is much more rigid so in time if you're using a Laptop can become damaged and the wires can come loose. Patch leads are designed to bend and flex.

You can purchase a smooth slimline outlet which looks very neat. I use an 'all-in-one' box with 2 or 4 Connectix 4000 outlets all-in-one one boxes. I have pictures of them in the 'connections' Chapter and they are the slimmest and neatest. Again available online. You may be able to buy other slimmer types if you want something even slimmer.

Patch Leads
These are simple leads that plug from the socket to the computer/Smart TV. They have RJ45 ends and you can buy them in any length – I'd go for 3 meters.

7. Equipment Needed to Move the Router

This is the same general tool selection that you'll need as hard-wiring. Again this is the best case scenario of tools and I'm sure once you've looked at the job, worked out your cable route, you will discover you don't need half of this equipment. Most of this equipment is available at your local hardware shop or online, or even perhaps you can borrow the odd tool from a friend over a weekend to complete the work.

Basic Tools:
(Available from any tool centre)
Wire Cutters
Flat-blade Screwdriver
Phillips (cross-head) Screw Driver
Hammer - WHITE and BLACK cable clips

Raw plugs
Screws

Punch Down Tool connection tool (connecting the modules)

Battery Drill
Masonry drill bit – 5mm
Wood Drill bit – 5mm

Power Drill (SDS is usually the best)
Mix of heavy Masonry drill bits

Clip-gun - plus clips
BLACK and CLEAR pack of Tie-Wraps
Electrical Tape - WHITE and BLACK

Step Ladder
Double/Triple extension Ladder - if you have two floors (these can be hired and are very inexpensive)

Cable:
4 Pair Telephone Cable. You can use 2 pair cable or even 3 pair cable but I've always used 4 pairs. Although a phone socket is 'looping on' from a working socket and will only use 2 wires (1 pair) it allows me the potential of using 3 other different pairs for different things. An additional line for example. Also i have in some cases found the pair I'm using has been damaged for whatever reason, for example a carpet fitter etc that came after me. So having breathing space for any eventuality is always a great idea.

1 x Linejack/Telephone Master Socket - this is what we are installing.

8. Preparation

An engineer I worked with used to tell me that you should spend an hour looking around the job before you actually do ANY work. This saves massive amounts of wasted time launching into cabling and opening up routes which we may not even need.

Firstly look at where you want the new socket or where you want the Router.

Hard-Wiring

Hard-Wiring involves running a separate cable for your TV, computer, and/or Laptop. One cable per piece of equipment. Most Routers have capacity for 4 possible pieces of equipment. So in terms of cabling we are looking at routes from the Router to the new locations.

The Router

Moving the Router involves paralleling a socket from your main line socket to the new location. So we are in effect duplicating your main line running one cable to a more central position to where you are using your phones, laptops, and smart TV etc.

Possible Cable Routes

Can we cable internal or external? Can we sneak along a carpet or are we forced outside along a wall? Look at the surrounding walls - which wall can you get out of to the outside wall? Which wall are you going to site the sockets on? Which wall is easier to get outside? Walk around your house - You're looking for any cable routes that would help get you from your Router to your new computer socket - or from your main socket to your new socket.

Things that will help
Do you have access to your ground floor rooms through the basement? Do you have access to a wood floor that could be lifted easily?

Some houses have basements that you can literally walk through and drill through the floor to where you need the socket if your new socket is on the ground floor.

Attic

The attic is another good location, again if the roof spans the whole house you can use this as your method to cable to the various rooms and drop down through the eves and down the outside of the house. Then go in through the wall.

Power
You want to avoid cabling right next to power as this can cause interference with data transmission.

9. Cabling from the Router - Data Sockets

When I went to a client's house to install more phone and data sockets neatness was of paramount importance. In many cases they didn't want to see any cables. You obviously can't magic cables inside walls but there are many tricks to help conceal and hide cables and use the house to your advantage.

Instead of me going through every possible scenario and how to overcome it, I'm going to break it down into simple situations. I will assume you have or don't have access to the roof, same with the basement and outside wall. Internally being the last resort, if that is all you have then you will have to use that. For example if you live in a flat where you have no attic, no basement, and no walls then there is still an option. So without further ado let's get started.

Access to Basement
If you have access through a basement and you can get to your Router and the new socket position, then this is the best-case scenario. The best thing about this place is we have access to all of the ground floor or at least most of it. So I would drill down from the Router position - cable through the basement and then drill down again where you want the new socket. Then i would poke the cable up.

Tip
Tape the cable to a small rod to assist going through the hole. Something like a metal coat hanger cut and bent straight is perfect.

Try to avoid drilling into beams as these are very thick. You will be drilling through wood most likely so will need a sharp wood drill bit (available from a hardware shop) and a battery drill.

Once you have the cable at both ends you can use a clip-gun or hammer and clips and bang the cable into the wood beans in the basement. Pull the cable taut so it's neat and tight.

Access to Attic
This is another great place to utilize for running a cable through. So the problem here to how to get into and get out of the roof.

Depending on how high your roof is – 1 or 2 floors you will need a ladder/step-ladder and someone to hold it for you.

So we need to firstly exit the house by drilling ideally at low level out through the wall and ideally from the Router. This avoids any internal cabling straight away.

Most main line sockets are situated on an outside wall so you maybe able to poke a cable back out the same hole. If not a power dill with a masonry drill bit can handle this. Make sure you are horizontal with the drill bit and have checked where the drill will roughly exit. Also make sure you are not drilling near the existing cable as a drill bit will mangle it - so angle the bit away and try to leave as a much room as possible.

So we made it outside.

The next part is to get up into the roof. A cable being clipped up the wall can be a little unsightly so if this isn't possible the best place to go up is behind a drain-pipe. You can tie-wrap the cable up the drain pipe so it's at the eves level.

To get into the attic i would suggest poking a flat piece of trunking out from inside the roof - so it pokes out under the eves. This will be a little tricky but you should see some light from inside the roof and aim for that. To help you, someone could knock on the part of the roof you want to exit from so once you're in the roof you can find the right area. A dust mask maybe a good idea working in the attic!

Once you see the trunking poke out from the roof you can tape it onto the trunking and pull it inside.

Cabling across the attic roof is fairly straight forward and we can exit the roof in exactly the same way we entered it as near to the room with the new socket as possible. Again i would use some flat trunking lidding to poke out of the roof and tape the cable to this.

Here is an example of cabling entering and exiting a roof and utilizing an old route:

If you don't want to go through the roof you can actually come around the eves clipping it under the roof tiles using a clip-gun if you have one or the hammer and clips. Then down the side of the house to the room you want to install the socket into.

Again coming down behind a drainpipe is very neat.

Then you're looking to drill from the inside of the room to the outside wall. Ideally you want to drill above the skirting and site the data socket so that it covers the hole you have drilled. Then you can bring the cable down behind the drain-pipe and use a hammer and clips to cable to the hole in the wall.

Trick 1
Wire Coat-hangers that are cut, cutting off the hook and bent straight make great rods to poke through a thick wall. You can use electrical tape and tape the cable to it.

Trick 2
I have used a fake drain-pipe to conceal cables when the routing has been really awkward and this works a treat if you really don't want to see cables at all.

Using both Routes:
Also sometimes you may end up using both the attic and basement to get to awkward positions. If you're cabling from the basement left corner and you want your computer socket on the second floor of the right corner it may be easier to rise up behind a drainpipe and get into the roof void – go across the roof attic and drop down. If this is the case, I would cable the roof first and drop down so you're not fighting gravity.

No access to roof or Basement:
This is relatively frequent and means you're into drilling out an outside wall and surface cabling either at low level or high level on the eves. Once you can't hide cables you're really into surface cabling. Ideally you want to get up high to the eves and cable along the wood. You can buy cat5e in black which maybe neater than the typical Grey color it comes in. When a black cable is tautly clipped it can look very neat. If you don't have far to cable at ground level then it may make sense to drill out and cable along low level. Again clipping tautly will look neat.

Using the Carpet:

If none of these are options are available then the other possibility is using the carpet to hide cables. When you pull a carpet up there is a small gap between the gripper and the wall. This is a great place to hide 1 cable. You can also pull up the gripper. I would ease it up with 2 flat-blade screwdrivers. Then hammer it down giving yourself some extra room.

For this work you will need a chisel to take notches out of door frames just to give you some extra space for the door to close. You need to take special care that you have allowed enough room for the carpet to go back and the door can open and close properly without pinching or damaging the cable.

You can use a variety of these options and there's always a route through a house, it may just take some extra time planning it.

So let's get up and go and check out our routes and get cabling.

10. Moving the Router - A New Socket

As I've stated neatness is king. You obviously can't magic cables inside walls but there's many tricks to help conceal and hide cables and use the house to your advantage.

Instead of me going through every possible scenario and how to overcome it, I'm going to break it down into simple situations. I will assume you have or don't have access to the roof, same with the basement and outside wall. Internally being the last resort, if that is all you have then you will have to use that. For example if you live in a flat where you have no attic, no basement, and no walls then there is still an option. So without further ado let's get started.

Above is the main socket and we will be running one cable from this.

Access to Basement
This is the best-case scenario. The best thing about this place is we have access to all of the ground floor or at least most of it. This would probably be moving the router to a more central location within the house on the ground floor. So I would drill down from where you want your socket through the floor into the basement. Try to avoid drilling into a beam as these are very thick. You will be drilling through wood most likely so will need a wood drill bit (available from a hardware shop) and a battery drill.

I would then drop the cable down the hole rather than poking it up. You can do the same for the existing line socket - again drilling down. So you can run the cable between the two.

Access to Attic

This is another great place to utilize for running a cable through. So the problem here to how to get into and get out of the roof.

Depending on how high your roof is – 1 or 2 floors you will need a ladder/step-ladder and someone to hold it for you.

So we need to firstly exit the house by drilling ideally at low level out through the wall. Most main line sockets are situated on an outside wall so you may be able to poke a cable back out the same hole. If not a power dill with a masonry drill bit can handle this. Make sure you are horizontal with the drill bit and have checked where the drill will roughly exit. Also make sure you are not drilling near the existing cable as a drill bit will mangle it - so angle the bit away and try to leave as a much room as possible.

So we made it outside.

The next part is to get up into the roof. A cable being clipped up the wall can be a little unsightly so the best place to go up is behind a drain-pipe.

To get into the attic you will need to get into the eves. I would suggest poking a flat piece of trunking out from inside the roof - so it pokes outside. This will be a little tricky but you should see some light from inside the roof and aim for that. To help you, someone could knock on the part of the roof you want to exit from so once you're in the roof you can find the right area. A dust mask maybe a good idea working in the attic!

Once you see the trunking you can then get the cable up the wall and tape it onto the trunking. You can use black tie-wraps to hold the cables to the drain-pipe and conceal them behind it.

Cabling across the attic roof is fairly straight forward and we can exit the roof in exactly the same way we entered it as near to the room with the new socket as possible.

Here is an example of cabling entering and exiting a roof and utilizing an old route:

If you don't want to go through the roof you can actually come around the eves clipping it under the roof tiles using the clip-gun if you have one or the hammer and clips. Then down the side of the house to the room you want to install the socket into.

Again coming down behind a drainpipe is very neat.

Then you're looking to drill from the inside of the room to the outside wall. Ideally you want to drill above the skirting and site the telephone jack so that it covers the hole you have drilled. Then you can bring the cable down behind the drain-pipe and use a hammer and clips to cable to the hole in the wall.

Trick 1
Wire Coat-hangers that are cut, cutting off the hook and bent straight make great rods to poke through a thick wall. You can use electrical tape and tape the cable to it.

Trick 2
I have used a fake drain-pipe to conceal cables when the routing has been really awkward and this works a treat if you really don't want to see cables at all.

Using both Routes:
Also sometimes you may end up using both the attic and basement to get to awkward positions. If you're cabling from the basement left corner and there is a telephone point needed on the second floor of the right corner it may be easier to rise up behind a drain-pipe and get into the roof void – go across the roof attic and drop down. If this is the case, I would cable the roof first and drop down so you're not fighting gravity.

No access to roof or Basement:

This is relatively frequent and means you're into drilling out an outside wall and surface cabling either at low level or high level on the eves. Once you can't hide cables you're really into surface cabling. Ideally you want to get up high to the eves and cable along the wood. When a black cable is tautly clipped it can look very neat. If you don't have far to cable at ground level then it may make sense to drill out and cable along low level. Again clipping tautly will look neat.

Using the Carpet:

If none of these are options are available then the other possibility is using the carpet to hide cables. When you pull a carpet up there is a small gap between the gripper and the wall. This is a great place to hide 1 cable. You can also pull up the gripper. I would ease it up with 2 flat-blade screwdrivers. Then hammer it down giving yourself some extra room.

For this work you will need a chisel to take notches out of door frames just to give you some extra space for the door to close. You need to take special care that you have allowed enough room for the carpet to go back and the door can open and close properly without pinching or damaging the cable.

You can use a variety of these options and there's always a route through a house, it may just take some extra time planning it.

So let's get up and go and check out our routes and get cabling.

11. Connecting a Data Cable

There's a number of ways to connect to both ends of our new data cable. One way is to crimp a RJ45 plug on either end of the cable and plug this straight into the Router and your Computer respectively. The other way is to mount a Cat5/Cat6 socket on a wall. You then use a patch lead at either end and connect to the Router and Computer.

Personally i like to use 'cable' to get from one point to another and lock it in place with sockets. Then use Patch leads which use 'strands' of copper wire inside the cores rather than a solid copper core used in cable. What this means is that a patch lead is far more flexible and is perfect for a laptop. Cable doesn't bend very well so if you're using this hard-wired link for a laptop which will receive a certain amount of movement then I definitely recommend mounting a back box.

Below you can see I have used two different types of back boxes which can both be bought online, just type in cat5e connection sockets online.

To mount your back box you will need a power drill, 2 plugs and 2 screws. Once you have screwed the back box to the wall we are ready to connect.

Here is the tool you will need which again comes in various forms:

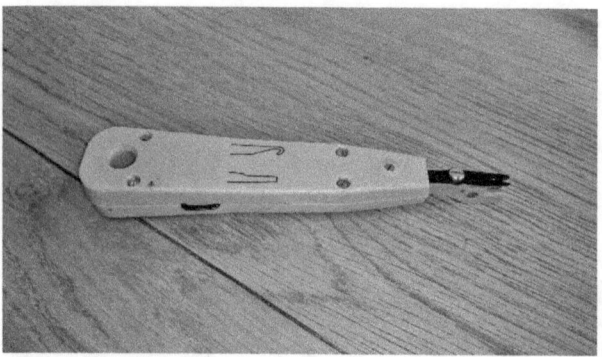

Here is the back of the module which you will need to connect to. The wires come in pairs, blue, orange, green and brown. The have a white leg and a colored leg. These have to be in the exact order that the colors designate on the module.

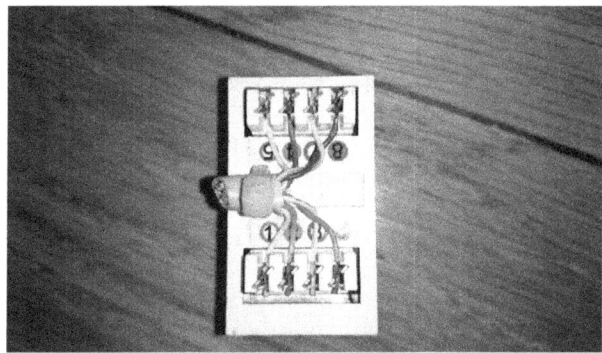

Finally this is what the socket should look like below.

Below is the 'all-in-one' socket lid and the inside of the data socket which you an also use. I prefer this because it is much slimmer.

As you can see this has potential for 4 cables which gives you scope for additional computers but you can buy a two port socket which is ideal.

Here is what the finished socket will look like.

RJ45 Connections

This is another option if you don't want to use any data sockets. The drawback is cable isn't supple and plugs can work loose if you're using a laptop that moves around on your desk or lap. If you want to use a crimp and RJ45 plugs then here's how you connect. First you obviously need a RJ45 crimper which crushes the wires inside a RJ45 plug - and the plugs themselves:

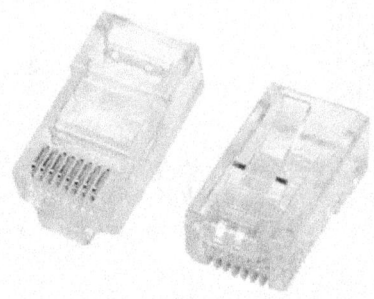

You need to strip the cable to about 2 centimetres. Then spread the wires out in this order:

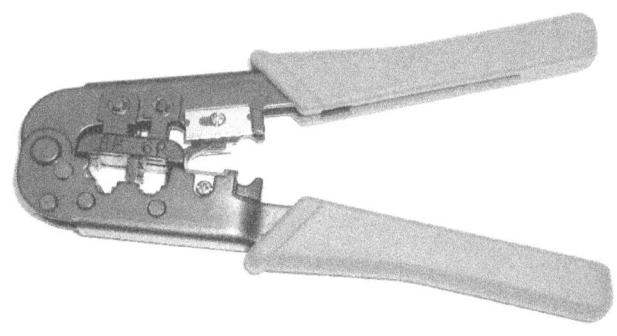

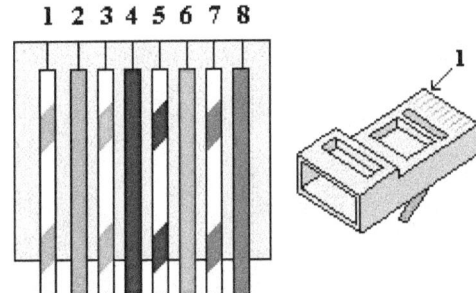

Then cut the wires to about 1.5 centimetres - With the RJ45 plug pins facing towards you - slide the wires into the RJ45 plug. Then use a crimper to crush the wires into place - I would do 3 good squeezes.

12. Connecting a Line Socket

Once you have mounted the back box on the wall with a drill, 2 plugs and 2 screws you will need to connect to the front plate.

Here is the tool you will need which again comes in various forms:

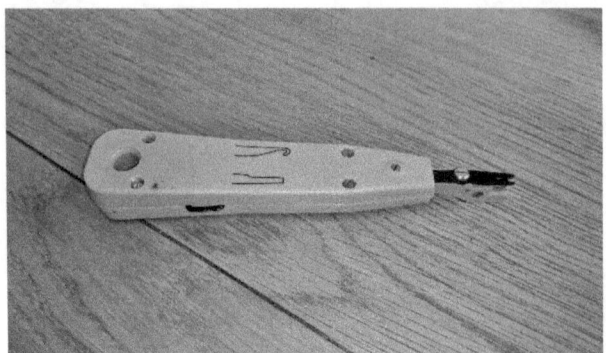

Below we have the cable stripped and ready to connect.

Below you can see i have connected the Blue-White to 5 and the White-Blue to 2 using the punch down tool.

I have then screwed the front plate back and this is ready to test.

Connecting up the live line end

So then we want to connect the live main socket now - below.

Remove the front module and again using the punch down tool connect the Blue-White to 5 and White-Blue to 2.

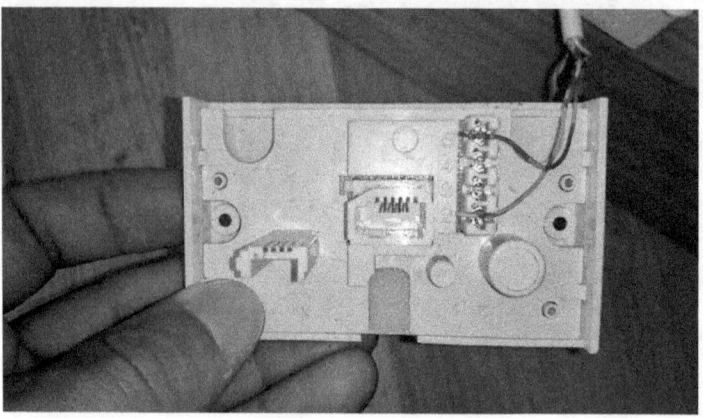

Then screw the plates back on to test.

13. Testing the Hard-Wired Socket

So once we have connected both ends we are ready to test. The best way is to simple plus it all in and try it out. There are scanners you can buy but for one cable it isn't worth it. If you can borrow one then it may be worth a go.

So below we can see the Router end. Use a patch lead to link your new socket and plug this into the first port on the Router.

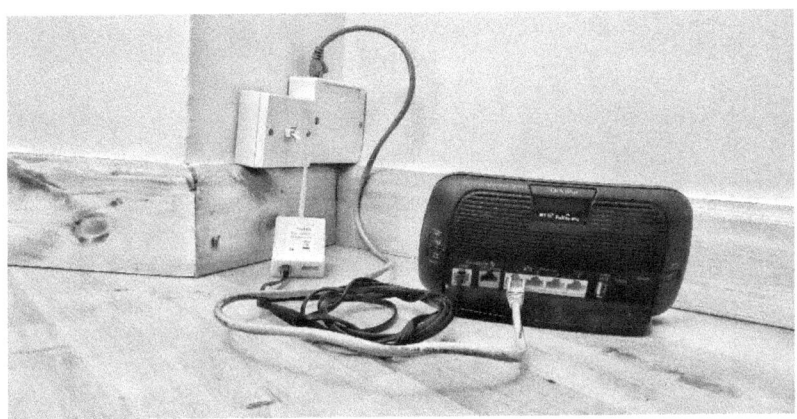

Below is the socket mounted on the wall. So use a long patch lead - 3 meters and you plug it into your computer/laptop.

If it works then fantastic, this means we are online! However first check you are using the hard-wire link and not still on Wi-Fi. You may need to go into your 'settings' to double to check.

If it's not connecting then:

- Make sure the connections on the modules are correct. If one wire is off or miss-connected then it won't work. So re-terminate all the connections both ends. Again make sure you're using the correct colors both ends. Sometimes in dark rooms the green can look like the blue and vice versa.
- Try a different socket on the Router
- Try different patch leads
- Make sure the Wi-Fi is still working and the Line is working

14. Testing the Router

So we have connected both ends and are ready to test!

Simply plug the ADSL splitter in first to the new socket otherwise the line will sound noisy. Then plug a house phone into the phone side of the ADSL Splitter. Pick up the handset - you should have dial-tone. Dial out to make sure you can make a call. Then using your mobile ring into the house to test it is ringing.

If it works then fantastic, this means we have a working line. If not make sure the connections are correct. If one wire is off or mis-connected then it won't work. So re-terminate all the connections. Again make sure you're using the correct colors both ends. If it's still not working try a different color pair. Sometimes in dark rooms the green can look like the blue and vice versa. Also change the ADSL filter as these have a tendency to be faulty too.

Then plug the Router into the Broadband side of the filter and power it up. The lights will tell you when it has connected to the Broadband - they usually all go blue - approx. 5minutes. Then you can use your tablet/smart phone to test the Wi-Fi which means it's connected.

Secondly now we have the Router in the correct place - ideally next to your computer you can now maximize the Broadband speed.

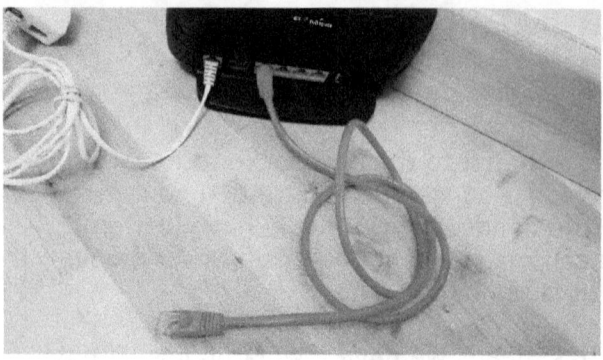

Simply plug a patch lead - as shown above into your computer. Some Laptops will have to be programmed in its settings to use the hard-wired connection. Then you are ready to use your Broadband speed to its max!

15. Faster and Finished!

We have reached the end of my guide on how to solve your Broadband speed problems and maximize the effectiveness of your Internet experience. I hope the information i have provided will be of use to you and given you a head start on maxing out your Broadband speed. Once you have a solid cable link, and/or moved your Router you should have less issues with speed and connection problems and be working at its optimal level.

Remember to consider safety first when using tools and ladders and ask for help when going up a ladder.

I have a number of other books I've written all linked to data networking and telecommunications. I have written about data networking your house, moving your Router, moving a telephone socket and even making money from data networking.

Thanks and goodbye!

--Martin

Get All The Books In The Series:
How To Boost Wi-Fi Speed: DIY Hacks To Increase Speed

How to move a Telephone Socket in your Home

www.ingramcontent.com/pod-product-compliance
Lightning Source LLC
Chambersburg PA
CBHW061234180526
45170CB00003B/1297